Meditative Prayers for Today

T0273387

In grateful memory of
Arthur and Violet Newton

MEDITATIVE PRAYERS FOR TODAY

Adam Bittleston

Floris Books

First published in 1953 by the Christian Community Press
This edition published 2017 by Floris Books
Second printing 2019

© The Christian Community, 1953, 1999

All rights reserved. No part of this publication may
be reproduced without the prior permission of
Floris Books, Edinburgh
www.florisbooks.co.uk

British Library CIP Data available
ISBN 978-178250-467-2
Printed in Poland through Hussar

Floris Books supports sustainable forest management
by printing this book on materials made from wood that
comes from responsible sources and reclaimed material

Contents

Introduction

Many of the prayers in this book were written more than thirty years ago. The spiritual climate was very different then: there was much less interest in meditation, and probably a good deal less interest in prayer, than there is now. The practice of meditation has largely developed outside the traditional Churches, often guided by Indian teachers, or teachers of Western birth drawing upon Eastern sources. The practice of prayer has mainly developed within the traditional Churches, particularly in the form of groups meeting for prayer. The increase in the practice of prayer springs frequently from the will to help others who are sick or in need, while many turn to meditation from a deeply justified longing for inner tranquillity and freedom from anxiety.

It may be useful to say something here about the distinction between meditation and prayer — though of course both words can be used with varying shades of meaning and are practised in widely diverse ways. But perhaps in nearly all forms of meditation there is a turning away from the external world which we encounter through the familiar senses — sight and hearing in particular — and from our problems in the immediate present. Many people who have tried to do this, perhaps very faithfully over years, suffer from a sense of failure; they seem, to themselves, to have achieved nothing. Others find at such moments that their horizons, both in space and in time, grow very much wider, in a way that is a deep relief to them. Perhaps with the help of words given by great teachers, they begin to find themselves in another realm of being, where there are no static objects, but only living beings and the powers that stream from them — and where nevertheless the deepest tranquillity is to be found. And there are many whose experience falls somewhere between these results — who have perhaps moments in meditation which seem promising, and others which seem quite barren. In this realm very great patience is needed.

In general, what may be called a meditative mood, a sense of tranquility and withdrawal from the immediate pressures of life, is the right preparation for prayer. There is a notable exception to this: sometimes very acute need or danger can give wings to prayer, in a way that fully is justified. But there are those who would say that the less a prayer contains any element of petition, the more it is simply a meditation and nothing else, the better it is. Yet what mars prayer may not be the presence of petition, but the qualities of self-seeking and short-sightedness which often enter this. Certainly the Lord's Prayer and the seventeenth chapter of St John's Gospel — the High-Priestly Prayer — are among the greatest prayers we can find anywhere, and both contain petitions; but these, if they are rightly understood, they have nothing selfish or short-sighted about them. In ordinary life, we also have to consider, if we want to ask for something, 'Is this request justified? If it is granted, will somebody else be deprived of something they need? May it not run counter to the deeper intentions of others, including the one to whom we are speaking?'

Not everyone who believes in meditation, or has even practised it faithfully for years, will necessarily be sure that private prayers are actually heard, that they reach any other consciousness than that of the one who prays. But meditation can be a very good preparation for gaining this conviction. While meditation may not imply that there is a hearer, petition implies that there is not only a hearer, but one able to help in the fulfilment of what is asked. From feeling the presence, when we meditate, of watchful spirits, for whom our consciousness is spread out, as a landscape is for earthly eyes, we go on to the conviction that such beings are not only observers, but can work within us, and in other human beings around us, when they are given the opportunity. For just as the clamour in our minds can prevent us from being aware of these beings at all, so the fears and doubts in us can impede them in their help. Prayer makes open a way for them into our world, and they are ready to use it.

In this book these beings are called by names used in Christian tradition — for example the name 'Angels.' For many today such names are quite meaningless. But it is not necessary to reject everything in the book for this reason. It may well be that this book comes into the hands of some for whom almost nothing in it quite makes sense; but it would still be useful if it stirred them to make prayers or meditative sayings for themselves. Words given from initiate wisdom should not be altered; but these prayers can readily be changed or shortened, or even a single line be used by itself. Readers who have no real picture of St Columba or St Elizabeth of Hungary, and yet wish to use 'Friday,' could simply omit them or put in other great human beings and qualities. For some people, for deep-seated reasons, the name 'Christ' is impossible; they can use other names for the patient, creative, loving Power at work in the universe.

There are good reasons for recalling, at the outset of a prayer or meditation, what place we have reached in the stream of time. The short rhythms of day, week and year reflect in miniature the great rhythms of the universe, of which we are aware in the depth of our souls. Simply to remember the time of day or the time of year — both of which express relationships between earth and sun — frees us a little from self-absorption.

It may well puzzle some readers of this book that in the sequence for times of the year a few *months* appear, while others — July and October, for instance — do not. The explanation is that the prayers for Advent, Epiphany, Lent, Midsummer and Michaelmas are thought of as four complete weeks after their beginning. Thus Advent covers December up to Christmas, Epiphany all January (from the 6th), Midsummer and Michaelmas most of July and October. Lent is thought of as four full weeks before Easter, which has itself a longer period, the forty days until Ascension. Christmas includes the twelve days from December 25 to January 5, and Ascension the ten days to Whitsun. For the purposes of this book, the Whitsun festival period can vary in length according to the date of Easter, so that it extends to June 23, the eve of St John.

This division of the year's course into festival periods and intervals between them accords in general with the practice of The Christian Community, the religious body in which the writer of these prayers has worked for nearly fifty years. Those who know it will recognize how much these prayers owe to its sacramental life, and to the influence of Rudolf Steiner, with whose help and guidance The Christian Community came into being in the autumn of 1922.

Finally, this book is not meant to be read straight through, but a little at a time, occasionally. May some of its words reach those who read them at moments of grief or bewilderment, and bring hope.

February 1982

Evening

I go into the realm of the invisible.
The weight of my earthly body,
The surging forces of my earthly life,
Release their hold.
In the world into which I now enter
The watchful care of Angels,
The loving guidance of the Archangels,
The creative power of the Spirits of the Ages,
Work upon human souls.
My heart bears in it many thoughts of conflict,
But also the thought of Christ.
May this grow in the world of sleep
Into full being —
That I receive through powers of Light
His strength and peace.

Morning

I come from the realm of the invisible,
And penetrate anew
The stream of my earthly life,
The house of my earthly body.
I thank the world of Spirit,
Which has held my soul.
I thank the world of earth,
Which has guarded my body.
May the Light of Christ
In the light of day
Shine for my soul
Upon paths of earth.
May the holy aims of God
Which have warmed my soul in sleep
Be remembered through the aid of Christ
In waking deeds.

Sunday

Before world-beginning
Christ shone in His glory,
Light of true Light,
One with the Father,
In all eternity,
Thou camest on earth,
Taking man's form,
Bearing man's fate,
Making life out of death,
Leading souls from the dark.
May we stand in Thy sight.

Monday

When we go out into the world as we
    have made it
Everywhere there speaks to us
Forgetfulness of the Spirit.
If human work were to be without love
The earth would become a bleak and
    barren desert.
Through forgetfulness of the Spirit
Love ebbs away.
Bring to mind in us, O Christ,
Inspirer of true human love,
How we have come to the earth
From the fields of light,
From the heights of the Spirit.
May we bring to the earth
What we have seen in the Spirit.
May remembrance of God
Grow strong in our souls
Overcoming the mists
Which hide the meaning
In the work of each day.

Tuesday

As light unites all beings of the world
So lives among us human speech.
But our speech today is heavy with guilt,
Guilt of indifference and unawareness,
Guilt of anger and pride.
Thy word, O Christ, encountered these;
They condemned Thee.
They live still in our word.
From our inmost hearts, O Christ,
Make new our speech.
When we speak with one another
May we remember
That we come from the Father,
And are led by Thee
To the awakening of the Holy Spirit,
Through the days and the weeks and the years.

Wednesday

Upon the temple of our body
Worked through the ages
The servants of God,
Mighty spiritual creators.
This is now my dwelling;
But it is darkened
By the power of tempters
To whom my soul has listened.
O Christ, against Thee
The voice of temptation
Could achieve nothing.
Thou art the Healer
For all our sickness.
Work in this body
That each of its elements,
Its warmth and its breath,
Its quickening blood,
The bones which sustain
The form which God gave,
Be hallowed by Thee.

Thursday

O Christ, Thou readest
The living book of human destiny.
In all who come to Thee
Thou knowest the inmost soul,
The body's need, the spirit's seeking.
In my thought of human beings
May I receive Thy light.
In my experience of human deeds
May I feel Thy will.
May we all, as Thy Community,
Find the right ways
For human souls
Who will to serve Thy Spirit.

Friday

Let me remember the servants of Christ,
Who kept on their hearts
His will for the world.
Beneath the Cross, the beloved disciple
Winning from pain eternal patience,
Beholding in darkness the new beginning.
Paul, who endured all persecution,
Rejoicing in the freedom of the Christian soul.
Columba, through the dark and the cold,
Journeying to build a faithful brotherhood.
Francis, overcoming the fear of leprosy,
And raising men's vision to the beauty of earth.
Elizabeth, bringing red roses
Into the depths of need.
The work of the servants of Christ
Holds in it sure promise
For the future of earth.
May we protect
What they have planted.
Their power live
In words and deeds of ours.

Saturday

O Christ, I remember with love and thankfulness
Those I have known
Who have passed through the gate of death.
I know that some of these have looked on my
    soul
From the realm in which their souls dwell.
I thank Thee for all I have received from them;
For Thou hast brought our lives to meet.
May my thoughts and feelings reach unto them,
    through Thee,
May they add warmth and purpose
To my earthly life.
And may my meeting again with them
Be blessed by Thee.

Easter I

Unto the sorrowing heart of Mary Magdalene
Thou camest in the garden of fresh life
That seeks in flower and tree the sunlit air.

Unto the questioning head of Thomas Didymus
Thou camest in the quiet upper room
By barred doors sheltered from the city's hatred.

Unto the faltering will of Simon Peter
Thou camest on the lake shore where
   he laboured
As fisher with his brethren on the waters.

And so Thou comest to our sorrowing heart
In the pure rhythms of the earth, sun, stars —
Linking our being's pulse to Paradise.

And so Thou comest to our questioning head
Revealing how the slain and buried Good
Takes on new body from the Invisible.

And so Thou comest to our faltering will,
Speaking to each of us our own true name,
Calling us from our graves to work with Thee.

Ascension

The clouds receive
The Risen Christ
That He may rule
The world of Life.

Witness of Him
We seek in earth
Where waters bear
The spirit's grace.

The moving air
And songs of birds
Say in the light
He has a home.

And blossoms feel
The loving flames
He sendeth them
As messengers.

Between men's hearts
Strengthen the love —
O Lord of bread,
Giver of wine!

That in the world
Thou fillest now
As Spirit-Sun,
We lift our sight!

Whitsun

Thou holy fire, making Thy home in us,
When we at peace can see and serve the truth,
Make strong in us the memory of Christ,
Bring to our tongues His world-renewing word.

Thou gracious light, uniting distant men
In certainty on paths of active thought,
Make clear to us the charge of destiny,
Bring to our heads Thy world-renewing hope.

Thou healing breath, who in the body's depths,
Restorest harmony with heaven's will,
Let live in us the order of the stars,
Bring to our hearts their world-renewing joy.

St John the Baptist

(Midsummer)

Thou herald spirit, by the Father's grace
Abiding witness to the Light of Lights,
Look on our seeking.

All we have done on earth has left its trace,
And all we say sounds on for spirit ears.
Help at our judging.

Baptizer of the waking soul, lead out
Our lives from barren conflict in the dark
Into Christ's presence.

Let sound the music of thy faithful heart,
Prophet of days to come, for brother men,
Unto Christ's glory.

August

Upon fields and orchards
Growing towards harvest
There look with blessing
The spirits of heaven;
And their gaze searches
Our hearts for ripening.
In the close weaving
Of manifold fates
They feel the pattern.
To the great Weaver,
The Lord of destiny,
We send our thoughts.
He heals the body,
The senses' dullness.
He wakes in the soul,
The spirit's will.
May His Community
Work in the world
Warmed by His grace —
Joining the sundered
Where at the altar
Our destinies meet.

September

Into the ripening
Of earth's great gifts
The mists of autumn
Begin to be woven.
We feel the touches
Of winter's coming.
The gentle earth
Has suffered conflict
Of man with man.
Dust is the witness
Of faithless hearts,
Of cruel thoughts.
May we learn
To care for the earth
Through the purpose of Michael,
Lord of the starry iron,
And the help of Raphael
Spirit of the morning dew.

Michaelmas

What is dull in our feeling,
What is hard in our thinking,
What fails in our willing,
We shall lift up
To fields of light,
Where the Archangel Michael,
Master over the Dragon,
Summons our thinking
To move in God's Glory,
Calls to our feeling
To live in God's Presence,
That we may waken
Our deepest will
To serve with him
The Son of God.

*The name of Michaël is three syllables,
which mean 'Who is like God?'*

November

Lord among the seven candles!
Giver of the light undarkened!
Helper of the souls who struggle
With their passions' bitter visage
On the wide stairs of the Night —

Thou who bearest from the Father
Sun-Life changeful and unchanging,
Healing for the spirit's weakness
When it weaves from wandering shadows
Error that denies Thy Being —

Christ whose love calls forth the roses
From the cross on which we suffer;
Guardian of the door to Heavens
Where the deeds on earth unfinished
Through God's grace prepare fulfilment —

Thy strong soul unite our feeling
With the souls of men who journey
From the earth to distant star worlds;
And with those who seek the entry
To the earth which Thou hast hallowed.

Advent

Thou mothering earth
Hast received the live seed
Into the dark
Good shelter of soil.
The mantle of night
Thrown wide over us,
And the sun as it goes
Its swift and short journey,
Speak to our hearts
In warning and promise.
Thou Earth hast borne up
The footsteps of Mary
Journeying patiently
Southwards to Bethlehem;
And the Earth bears us
Today in our travail,
That we may bring forth
Christ in our spirit.
So we may await Him
Sent by the Father,
Healer and bringer
Into our being
Of love without fail.

Christmas I

Across wild seas,
Through great forests,
Over barren mountains,
Men's souls are coming
To Thee, O Christ.
Led by troubled longing,
Led by the thirst for Light,
Led by desperate need.
The angel-song told the shepherds
In their quiet poverty
The way to the Child.
The star-radiance showed the kings
In their earnest wisdom
The way to the Child.
May the child in us follow the Way
Where the noise of the machine grows silent,
Where the shadow-show of print vanishes,
Where Nature redeemed rejoices,
About the Christ,
Who wakens our souls.
Where He is not seen
May we begin to show His Light;

Where He is not heard
May we begin to speak His Word;
May we find in souls
The will that seeks without fear
His will for the world.

A short Christmas prayer

Come, Child, into our hearts, and still the storm
Made by our selfish wishes wrestling there;
And weave again the fabric of mankind
Out of Thy Light, Thy Life, Thy loving Fire.

Christmas II

Voices in thunder from the bounds of heaven
Through age on age prepared the world of earth
To hold the form of man, whose inmost soul
Is born to serve the Christ.

His glory is about the humble child
Laid in the manger, bringing paradise
New among men who lift their hearts to see
The gift beyond all thought.

Bless Thou our troubled souls, grown poor
   in love,
From Thy eternal mercy which brings back
All that is lost into the fold of God,
O Word of worlds made man!

Epiphany

May the revelation of Christ
Shine out to the world,
Granting to the mind
Understanding
As clear gold.

May the love of Christ
Stream forth to souls,
Kindling in the heart
Prayer
As rising incense.

May the deeds of Christ
Be known by men's spirits,
Teaching in the hands
Devotion
As healing myrrh.

February

He who walked the paths of Galilee,
And streets of Jerusalem,
Has come among us
Everywhere on earth
Though our eyes may not see Him.
He shares man's grief,
He suffers man's conflict,
He breathes man's hope.
He seeks disciples
Who trust what can be seen
When the heart's light opens.
May we receive from Him
The life that sustains
Grace in the soul.
May He speak in our conscience
When we take up our work.
May He be our shepherd
When in the hours of sleep
We move in the Spirit.

Lent

Blind is the soul
Imprisoned deep
In weary flesh.

And spirit-will
Is wrenched away
From living good.

But we may tread
The road the Christ
Did follow then;

When all the wrong,
And all the pain
Were gathered up

That He, the Lamb,
Might bear for man
The bitter load,

And meet with man
The prince of hell
In the soul's night.

Easter II

By His strong thought forgetfulness of God,
By His strong love the hatred of good,
By His pure life the bitterness of death,
Are overcome in depths of earth.

Time is no longer empty, through His deed;
In our heart's beat His living grace awakes;
Into our house the Easter air is breathed
With joy that heals our blood.

Thou makest new our being that from God
Has made the long descent into the dark;
And as immortal brother Thou hast joined
The sojourners of earth.

Earth

Spirits of the Heights
Have sent their messengers:
Stones under our feet.
Upon the sustaining earth
May we be upright.

Spirits of the Heights
Have sent their messengers:
Flowers and trees around us.
Upon the living earth
May our hearts waken.

Spirits of the Heights
Have sent their messengers:
Birds and beasts about us.
Of all earth's offspring
May we be guardians.

Spirits of the Heights
Have sent their messengers:
Light and dark, life and death.
In all earth's changes
Christ may we find.

Against fear

May the events that seek me
Come unto me;
May I receive them
With a quiet mind
Through the Father's ground of peace
On which we walk.

May the people who seek me
Come unto me;
May I receive them
With an understanding heart
Through the Christ's stream of love
In which we live.

May the spirits who seek me
Come unto me;
May I receive them
With a clear soul
Through the healing Spirit's light
By which we see.

For one who has died

The Good Shepherd lead thee
Where thou art transformed
That thou mayest breathe
The air of eternal Being.

Where thou workest as soul
For worlds to come
The grace of the Spirit
Unite us with thee.

Intercessory prayer

Thou angel who keepest watch
Over the destiny of ...
Through waking and sleeping,
And the long ages of time:
May my thoughts, filled with hope,
Reach her (him) through Thee.
May she be strengthened
From the founts of will
Which bear us towards freedom.
May she be illumined
From the founts of wisdom
Which warm the inmost heart.
May she feel peace
From the founts of love
Which bless men's work.

Short intercession

May the Good Shepherd lead her (him)
Into peace of heart,
Into hopeful thinking,
Into patient strength of will;
Health of body,
Harmony of soul,
Clarity of spirit,
Now, and in the time to come.

In estrangement

May life still bring me
Times of good encounter,
Of help for one another,
Of increasing understanding,
With the one from whom I am now estranged.

For children between 3 and 14

May you grow
In joy before the wonders of the world,
In grief over the pain of others,
Beginning to hear
The call to help and to heal
According to the gentle light
Of the Angel who guards you.

In thought for a child

In thy breath the light of the sun
In thy bread the salt of earth
In thy ears true words of love
Sustain thy growing, changing life;
That thy spirit's will may work
That thy soul be warmed by joy
That thy body's world be built.

The guardian angel

Every pain endured,
Every word I speak,
Every wish and fear,
Every sense of joy,
My angel shares with me.

May your gentle warmth,
Angel, live afresh
Ever with new strength
From Christ who goes Himself
As Angel through the world.

Blessing on a house

(or at an evening meeting)

Measureless the starry heights,
Measureless the depths of earth,
And about us everywhere
Light-receiving, warmed by wonder,
Spirits weave man's destiny.
May the shelter of this house
Be a place of wakening
Peace within us, peace among us.

For a journey

The caring angel of my life
Sets out with me and holds the thread
At peace among my fellow-men.
Noise and illusion threaten me,
And yet the master of the loom is kindness,
And at arrival the warm angel waits.

For the peoples of the world

O Christ, Thou knowest
The souls and spirits
Whose deeds have woven
Each country's destiny.

May we who today
Share the world's life
Find the strength and the light
Of Thy servant Michael.

And our hearts be warmed
By Thy blessing, O Christ,
That our deeds may serve
The healing of peoples.

Grace before meals

The light has formed our food for earth,
And speech has formed the souls of men:
Eternal Light, eternal Word
Within our hearts be seen, be heard.

Thanksgiving

For the speaking light of the senses
Which bears into our souls
The world's abundance,
We thank the powers of heaven.

For the health that is in our bodies,
Even in illness and need,
Sustaining, renewing, refreshing,
We thank the will of Christ.

For the wonders of human friendship,
Which bless the life of earth
With the hope of eternal being,
We thank the Father's love.

A note on the Lord's Prayer

If anyone finds his way completely into the use of the Lord's Prayer, he may well feel that no other prayer is necessary for him. Every present need of mankind, and all hopes for the future, are contained within it.

But we are not always able to use it effectively. It is possible to approach it with all sincerity and yet meet with considerable difficulty; and it is possible to use it for years, and then find that we have somehow lost touch with its meaning.

Above all we need to bear in mind that the words of the Lord's Prayer are given to us by Christ Himself, and that each of them should be used as part of His language — as belonging in the context of what He said then to mankind, and of what He says now. If any word or sentence of the Lord's Prayer is lifeless to us, we need to understand and feel it afresh, by relating it to the fundamental purposes which Christ has for humanity; for we can learn what these purposes are.

We can think, for example, of three great qualities, which human beings can consciously train and develop in themselves: the capacities for wonder, compassion and conscientious action. Rudolf Steiner spoke particularly of these qualities as providing instruments for the effective work of Christ upon the earth; and we can see from experience that this is so.

One possible way in which we can deepen and renew our relationship to the Lords Prayer is by considering how the fulfilment of the petitions contained within it depends upon the development within humanity of these three qualities.

The Name of God can only be hallowed in the hearts of men through their power of wonder. If the world is dominated by a kind of knowledge which fails to awaken enough reverence, then the Name of God will be given meanings which are too narrow and personal. Nature and history have to be seen and known in ways which reach through the surface of things to the divine creative work; only through this can human speech be purified in the way implied by the Lord's Prayer.

The Kingdom of God will come about through the development of genuine mutual compassion, in which is included the desire to protect each other's freedom. Within every community, small or great, to which we may belong, there is the opportunity to share in the development of this compassion, through which the joy of one can become everyone's joy, and the grief of one can become everyone's grief, without any intrusion into individual privacy. Today when we care deeply for another person, we often find it difficult not to urge them in directions which we think will be for their good; but we can look forward to the development of a mood within Christian communities through which it will become natural to wait for the maturing, within each individual, of his own freely given inner law, in the sense described in the Sermon on the Mount.

Held together by mutual compassion, and moved by compassion for the needs of the world as a whole, true communities can begin to fulfil the Will of God, 'as it is in heaven, so also on the earth.' The ultimate guide here is the voice of conscience; not anything derived from convention or outer influences, but the speech of that part of our being which is born 'not of blood, nor of the will of the flesh, nor of the will of man, but of God.' The Will of the Father is done where true needs of every creature, for which He has made room in the world, are respected and fulfilled.

In the following three petitions, practical fields are described in which these great aims can be served. Where conscience works, all kinds of Bread, everything that nourishes the being of man, will be rightly shared. We should not rely on governments to see that this happens; the vigilance of each individual, both for his immediate environment and for the remotest parts of the world, is needed. We can see how this sort of concern is gradually becoming accepted as natural in our time.

Through compassion, we can hope to learn the difficult art of forgiveness towards others, and thereby open ourselves to receive the creative forgiveness which continually streams to us from heaven, through the course of our earthly destiny.

The words, 'Lead us not into temptation,' are often felt as a peculiar difficulty in the Lord's Prayer. 'Temptation' is the testing of our spiritual purpose under pressure of our wishes and emotions. We can indeed be led into this testing if we trust too much to our own personal powers of resistance; or if, allowing wishes to master us, we have to experience something of the darkness into which they would eventually lead. The power of wonder leads us in the opposite direction, away from the violence of desire; showing us the greatness of what is already being given, it teaches patience towards the wishes that are yet unfulfilled.

But it is possible for man to make a fundamentally different choice. He can reject wonder, compassion and conscience, and let himself be filled instead with the will to destroy. Something of this will lurk in nearly all men, generally very much disguised, for instance as apathy or despair. It is 'the Evil,' of which the last petition speaks. Complete inner freedom is only possible when the soul is no longer in any danger of being possessed by evil. Just as the Gospels describe in the Mother of Jesus the new Eve, in whose soul temptation can take no hold, so in the Beloved Disciple is indicated the human being in whose 'I' the will to betray or deny can find no place. He has gone through the death of the jealous, assertive, every-day self and received his true, innermost Self from Christ. 'Deliver us from Evil' asks that this process of redemption at the very centre of man's being may happen more and more.

The whole of the Lord's Prayer can be experienced like a sunrise. But it is not simply the earth receiving light from outside; the earth itself begins to become radiant, in sevenfold glory. Any particular thoughts which we use to help us in bringing the words of the Prayer to life are in the end to vanish within the flood of healing, gentle Light, into which we are led. Here the word 'we' can itself be given for the first time its complete meaning. Its use before has only been shadowy and provisional.

It is the task of all meditative prayer to prepare us for the falling away of illusion — to the accomplishment here on earth of St Paul's hope: 'For now we see in a glass darkly, but then face to face. Now I know in part; then I shall understand fully, even as I have been fully understood.' (1Cor.13:12) The heaven, of which the Lord's Prayer says that it is the home of the Father, is not only above and beyond all that we experience on earth; it is also within everything we know, as the glory of the Father's understanding, in which He would have us share.